IMMATERIAL GIFTS:
A SCRIPTURAL DEEP DIVE INTO GOD'S GIFTS TO US

…HOW MUCH MORE WILL YOUR HEAVENLY FATHER GIVE GOOD GIFTS TO THOSE WHO ASK HIM?
(MATTHEW 7:11)

HAVE YOU EVER RECEIVED A MATERIAL ITEM YOU'VE ALWAYS WANTED, JUST TO FIND OUT THAT IT LEAVES YOU FEELING EMPTY IN JUST A MATTER OF MONTHS, WEEKS, OR EVEN DAYS? HAVE YOU EVER WONDERED WHICH GIFTS FROM GOD ARE ETERNAL AND FULFILLING? THIS BOOK WILL DIRECT YOU TO SCRIPTURE, TO GIVE INSIGHT STRAIGHT FROM GOD'S OWN WORDS.

BY

SHANNON KLEIN

PROLIFIC KINGDOM PUBLISHING

Copyright © 2024 by Shannon Klein

All rights reserved. No part of this book may be reproduced or used in any manner without the written permission of the copyright owner except for the use of quotations in a book review or article.

Holy Bible, New Living Translation, Copyright © 1996, 2004, 2015 by Tyndale House Foundation. Used by permission of Tyndale House Publishers, Inc., Carol Stream, Illinois 60188. All rights reserved.

The Holy Bible, English Standard Version (ESV) is adapted from the Revised Standard Version of the Bible, copyright Division of Christian Education of the National Council of the Churches of Christ in the U.S.A. All rights reserved.

Copyright © 2015 by The Lockman Foundation, La Habra, CA 90631. All rights reserved. For Permission To Quote information visit http://www.lockman.org/

Scripture taken from the New King James Version®. Copyright © 1982 by Thomas Nelson. Used by permission. All rights reserved.

Scripture taken from the NEW AMERICAN STANDARD BIBLE®, Copyright © 1960, 1962, 1963, 1968, 1971, 1972, 1973, 1975, 1977, 1995 by The Lockman Foundation. Used by permission.

The Holy Bible, Berean Study Bible, Copyright © 2016, 2018, 2019 by Bible Hub. All Rights Reserved Worldwide.

———————

First Paperback Edition: December 2024

Published by: Prolific Kingdom Publishing

Cover Design: Shannon Klein

Edited/Formatted by: Prolific Kingdom Publishing

ISBN: 978-1-7340215-5-4

Dedicated To:

This book is dedicated to all the people I've met over this last year in Las Vegas. I believe God is doing something incredible in this city, and I'm happy to have been part of it. I've seen radical life transformations and next is tremendous spiritual growth in the hearts of those who live here. This is just the beginning!

My prayer is that you all continue to seek the Lord with sound doctrine. I wrote this book for you. May the words of God straight from the source penetrate through your minds to your spirit and radiate all throughout the land. May this equip you to go out and make disciples and continue the work God has called us to do.

Love, Shannon.

Foreword:

It is an honor to know Shannon Klein and to call her a sister in Christ and daughter of the Most High God. She is a diamond in the ruff, a treasure polished by God in the furnace of affliction. We often look at a Beautiful smile and have no idea of the price that person paid to be an overcomer. Proverbs 31:10 says, "Who can find a virtuous woman? For her price is far above rubies.." Shannon embodies the attributes of the Kingdom of God.

Even as she describes those attributes in this wonderful book, the Fruits of the Spirit are visibly displayed in her life. She displays the heart of Queen Esther for a new generation of believers. With the heart of a warrior, Shannon champions worship wherever she goes. Always looking to give her God praise, she loves to magnify her Father God, her Savior Jesus, and her Wonderful Counselor, Holy Spirit. From the moment I met her, I knew that she was different, like a rare flower, fearfully and wonderfully made.

Her awareness of God, His presence, and His Gifts sets her apart. Separated, Sanctified, and Set Apart for such a time as this. As you read this book, join Shannon on a journey to become more aware of the Immaterial Gifts that God has blessed us to walk in on a daily basis. Open your spiritual senses, elevate beyond the subconscious mind into the superconscious, and enter the supernatural treasures available to us from the Holy Spirit. John 4:24 says, "God is a spirit, and those who worship Him must worship Him in Spirit and in Truth."

His fruit, detailed in Galatians 5:22-23 and His Gifts, detailed in 1 Corinthians 12:1-11, are freely given to those who seek them out. But as Shannon mentions in this powerful book, we need to be hungry for them. Holy Spirit is saying ready when you are! He graciously waits like a gentleman, with all the power of eternity in His hands. He gently nudges us out of our comfort zone and into our identity, our purpose, and our destiny. Shannon details in this wonderful book how not to just exist but to use the gifts that God has given us to live life and it more abundantly.

Blessings and Favor,

Dr. John C. Whitfield III
CEO Prolific Kingdom

Preface

Being confident of this very thing, that He who began a good work in you will complete it until the day of Jesus Christ.

Philippians 1:6

God has already begun a good work in you, that's why you are reading this book. Either you stumbled on it or, perhaps, a friend gave it to you. Either way, God knew it would end up in your hands. I believe the scriptures in this book will nourish many gifts in you. Gifts of faith, joy, peace, hope, love, a sound mind, healing, wisdom, strength, and, most importantly, Salvation.

Introduction *1*

Chapter 1: Salvation *3*

Chapter 2: Faith *11*

Chapter 3: Joy *25*

Chapter 4: Peace *33*

Chapter 5: Hope *39*

Chapter 6: Love *45*

Chapter 7: Sound Mind *53*

Chapter 8: Healing *61*

Chapter 9: Wisdom *77*

Chapter 10: Strength *89*

Final *95*

About the Author *97*

Introduction

The greatest gifts we can ever acquire in life are neither diamonds, watches, nor cars, but rather immaterial attributes given to us by the Holy Spirit once we receive Jesus into our hearts as Lord and Savior. These gifts are ours as we gain access to them by His grace. These gifts grow as they are watered by the word, our humility, and even by each other.

Immaterial Gifts is a scriptural deep dive into some of the many blessings of God. He loves to give good gifts to His children. These are free and forever. They are fulfilling beyond anything that this world has to offer. No material item can ever compare to what is so readily available to us according to His promises and goodness.

Each gift is unique, yet they all exemplify His holy nature. This book will gift you an increased understanding and revelation of what it means to receive and develop these all. As you grow in the Lord, may His abundant love and mercy water the seeds of spiritual gifts that I pray this book will sow into your heart and soul.

Chapter 1

Salvation

The most important gift of all is the gift of salvation. Personally, I'd rather go to Heaven than not. I'm sure we can all agree on that. Thanks to Jesus, it's so simple! Yet, this statement alone can cause many emotions to be stirred up. I hope to simply break it down through Scripture, because why not use more of God's perfect words and less of my own?

"For I am not ashamed of the gospel of Christ, for it is the power of God to salvation for everyone who believes." (Romans 1:16)

Salvation

"For God so loved the world that He gave His one and only Son, that whoever believes in Him shall not perish but have eternal life. For God did not send His Son into the world to condemn the world, but to save the world through Him. Whoever believes in Him is not condemned, but whoever does not believe stands condemned already because they have not believed in the name of God's one and only Son." (John 3:16-18)

"If you declare with your mouth, "Jesus is Lord," and believe in your heart that God raised Him from the dead, you will be saved. For it is with your heart that you believe and are justified, and it is with your mouth that you profess your faith and are saved." (Romans 10:9-10)

"Believe in the Lord Jesus, and you will be saved." (Acts 16:13)

"Good People" don't go to Heaven.

Such a common misconception is this deceiving idea that being "good" will get one into Heaven. It is completely contradictory to the word of God. The Bible explicitly states how we enter into Heaven – by Him alone. As sinful human beings in a fallen world, any "goodness" we can do on our own will always be a mere shadow of what God's ultimate requirements are. Thankfully, He has given us grace to transcend this state and be saved.

"For it is by grace you have been saved, through faith—and this is not from yourselves, it is the gift of God—not by works, so that no one can boast." (Ephesians 2:8-9)

If we were to be judged by our works, that would be pretty terrible news for us, since none of our works are Holy enough.

"I will expose your righteousness and your works, and they will not benefit you." (Isaiah 57:12)

"For all have sinned and fall short of the glory of God." (Romans 3:23)

Jesus is *the* only way.

Jesus answered, "I am the way and the truth and the life. No one comes to the Father except through me." (John 14:6)

"Salvation is found in no one else, for there is no other name under Heaven given to mankind by which we must be saved." (Acts 4:12)

There is no other option.

"But all who reject me and my message will be judged on the day of judgment by the truth I have spoken." (John 12:48)

"Choose this day whom you will serve." (Joshua 24:15)

"Yet you refuse to come to me to have life." (John 5:40)

"Whoever transgresses and does not abide in the doctrine of Christ does not have God. He who abides in the doctrine of Christ has both the Father and the Son." (2 John 1:9)

"Enter through the narrow gate. For wide is the gate and broad is the road that leads to destruction, and many enter through it. But small is the gate and narrow the road that leads to life, and only a few find it." (Matthew 7:13-14)

"For the message of the cross is foolishness to those who are perishing, but to us who are being saved, it is the power of God." (1 Corinthians 1:18)

Hell is real.

"Don't be afraid of those who want to kill your body; they cannot touch your soul. Fear only God, who can destroy both soul and body in hell." (Matthew 10:28)

"Then the King will turn to those on the left and say, 'Away with you, you cursed ones, into the eternal fire prepared for the devil and his demons." (Matthew 25:41)

"And they will go away into eternal punishment, but the righteous will go into eternal life." (Matthew 25:46)

"But for those who are self-seeking and who reject the truth and follow evil, there will be wrath and anger." (Romans 2:8)

"He will punish those who do not know God and do not obey the gospel of our Lord Jesus. They will be punished with everlasting destruction and shut out from the presence of the Lord and from the glory of His might on the day He comes to be glorified in His holy people and to be marveled at among all those who have believed." (2 Thessalonians 1:9-10)

Warning – do not dilute the Gospel.

"My people are destroyed for lack of knowledge." (Hosea 4:6)

Jesus said, "I didn't make this up. What I teach comes from the One who sent me. Anyone who wants to do His will can test this teaching and know whether it's from God or whether I'm making it up. A person making things up tries to make himself look good. But someone trying to honor the one who sent him sticks to the facts and doesn't tamper with reality." (John 7:16-18)

"For the word of God *is* living and powerful, and sharper than any two-edged sword, piercing even to the division of soul and spirit, and of joints and marrow, and is a discerner of the thoughts and intents of the heart." (Hebrews 4:12)

"So, because you are lukewarm and neither hot nor cold, I will spit you out of my mouth." (Revelation 3:16)

"Now, the Spirit expressly says that in later times, some will depart from the faith by devoting themselves to deceitful spirits and teachings of demons." (1 Timothy 4:1)

"You are the salt of the earth, but if salt has lost its taste, how shall its saltiness be restored? It is no longer good for anything except to be thrown out and trampled under people's feet." (Matthew 5:13)

"Not everyone who says to me, 'Lord, Lord' will enter through the kingdom of Heaven. Many will say to me on that day, 'Lord, Lord, did we not prophesy in your name and in your name drive out demons and in your name perform many miracles?' Then I will say to them, 'Depart from me, I never knew you.'" (Matthew 7:21-23)

It is so important to take Jesus' words seriously. He is unique in that He is the only one who says He is right and everyone else is wrong. That's a wildly bold statement that should make us think. One cannot believe in Him and also believe in anything else. It's worth considering because what if He is right? Wouldn't that be something to take very seriously?

And you will know the truth, and the truth will set you free. (John 8:32)

"I and the Father are one." (John 10:30)

It is impossible to add or subtract from these truths. Doing so is to void the Gospel entirely. We can have freedom from bondage in this life and eternal salvation with one simple prayer!

Prayer:

Jesus, come into my life. Be my Lord and Savior. Forgive me of my sins and make me brand new. I want to follow You and allow You to heal and deliver me. Thank You for this free gift of salvation. In Jesus' name, I pray, amen.

Chapter 2

Faith

Faith is a gift.

"Looking unto Jesus, the author and finisher of our faith." (Hebrews 12:2)

"To those who through the righteousness of our God and Savior Jesus Christ have received a faith as precious as ours." (2 Peter 1:1)

The precious gift of faith was created and is completed and perfected by Jesus. It is not something that we can earn, nor do we deserve. It is freely given to us; it pleases God, leads us into salvation, and ultimately helps us walk into the full calling God has created for us.

Faith and Salvation:

Faith is intrinsically connected to salvation. You can't have one without the other. Faith is a gift that leads to salvation and is simultaneously produced by salvation.

"But we do not belong to those who shrink back and are destroyed, but to those who have faith and are saved." (Hebrews 10:39)

"For it is by grace you have been saved, through faith—and this is not from yourselves, it is the gift of God—not by works, so that no one can boast." (Ephesians 2:8-9)

I included this verse again-, to show how the two works in conjunction with each other.

"For everyone who has been born of God overcomes the world. And this is the victory that has overcome the world – our faith." (1 John 5:4)

What is faith?

Perhaps the most detailed description of faith is found in Hebrews chapter 11:

"Now faith is the substance of things hoped for, the evidence of things not seen. For by it, the elders obtained a good report. Through faith, we understand that the worlds were framed by the word of God, so that things which are seen were not made of things which do appear." (Hebrews 11:1-3)

Faith is not what we can see, yet it is critical to our foundation as believers and to the existence of the universe itself. In fact, without it, we cannot come to God. We wouldn't even be here in the first place if we came about by something already visible. It is only through the unseen hand of God that anything around us exists, and it is His same hand that guides us along the path of faith. Faith is not just hopeful, wishing, or trusting in some unknown force that is cold and impersonal. Faith is the path of following and trusting a living, personal God who rewards us by revealing more of Himself to us every day throughout our entire lives, walking with Him.

How we obtain faith:

"Faith comes by hearing, and hearing by the word of God." (Romans 10:17)

We must read and speak the word of God to receive the gift of faith. People who struggle with doubt often express that they just wish they had more faith. Faith is a gift that is easily activated. The great news is that there is no limit or cost to obtaining faith, as we have the Bible ready and available to us always. When we begin by telling the Lord that we will trust Him and seek Him out although we might not see or feel Him at that moment, we begin the lifelong adventure of walking through life with a living God who will show Himself to us in very personal ways all the days of our lives. Faith is not just stepping into the unknown and hoping for the best; it is having assurance that the God we serve and seek is real and He will reveal Himself to us and reward us in ways that will not only delight, but also surprise us as His presence and joy grows within us forever.

Why faith is important:

Faith pleases God and brings us into alignment with His plan for our lives.

"But without faith, it is impossible to please Him: for he that cometh to God must believe that He is, and that He is a rewarder of them that diligently seek Him." (Hebrews 11:6)

The rest of Hebrews chapter 11 gives several accounts of how important historical leaders inherited promises and salvation through faith. They were able to accomplish the will of God and walk fully into their callings because they utilized the gift of faith.

It was by faith that Abel brought a more acceptable offering to God than Cain did. Abel's offering gave evidence that he was a righteous man, and God showed His approval of his gifts. Although Abel is long dead, he still speaks to us by his example of faith.

It was by faith that Enoch was taken up to Heaven without dying – he disappeared because God took him. For before he was taken up, he was known as a person who pleased God.

It was by faith that Noah built a large boat to save his family from the flood. He obeyed God, who warned him about things that had never happened before. By his faith, Noah condemned the rest of the world, and he received the righteousness that comes by faith.

It was by faith that Abraham obeyed when God called him to leave home and go to another land that God would give him as his inheritance. He went without knowing where he was going. And even when he reached the land God promised him, he lived there by faith—for he was like a foreigner, living in tents.

So, too, did Isaac and Jacob, who inherited the same promise. Abraham was confidently looking forward to a city with eternal foundations, a city designed and built by God.

"It was by faith that even Sarah was able to have a child, though she was barren and was too old. She believed that God would keep His promise." Hebrews (11:4-5, 7-11)

These accounts are merely a fraction of the biblical stories of great men and women led by faith. In the same way, we, too, must live our lives according to faith.

Faith guides us.

"For we walk by faith, not by sight." (2 Corinthians 5:7)

"Your word is a lamp to my feet and a light to my path." (Psalm 119:105)

Since faith comes by the word of God, we are led by the word of God, which produces the faith that guides us. It is all connected.

Faith makes all things possible.

And Jesus said to him, "If you can believe, all things are possible to him who believes." (Mark 9:23)

"For with God nothing shall be impossible." (Luke 1:37)

Jesus answered them, "Truly, I say to you, if you have faith and do not doubt, you will not only do what has been done to the fig tree, but even if you say to this mountain, 'Be taken up and thrown into the sea,' it will happen." (Matthew 21:21)

So, the Lord said, "If you have faith as a mustard seed, you can say to this mulberry tree, 'Be pulled up by the roots and be planted in the sea,' and it would obey you." (Luke 17:6)

Then Jesus said to him, "Go your way; your faith has made you well." And immediately, he received his sight and followed Jesus on the road. (Mark 10:52)

"And Stephen, full of faith and power, did great wonders and miracles among the people." (Acts 6:8)

It is pretty incredible when we fully comprehend the power that faith carries. Miracles can be worked through us, when we put our faith in Jesus.

Faith is a choice.

"I have chosen the way of faithfulness; I have set my heart on your laws." (Psalm 119:30)

"Have faith in God," Jesus answered. (Mark 11:22)

"Watch, stand fast in the faith, be brave, be strong." (1 Corinthians 16:13)

"Above all, taking the shield of faith with which, you will be able to quench all the fiery darts of the wicked one." (Ephesians 6:16)

We can choose to walk in faith, put our faith in God, be steadfast in our faith, and take it up as a shield of protection against spiritual attack from the enemy.

Faith can be tested.

"My brethren, count it all joy when you fall into various trials, knowing that the testing of your faith produces patience. But let patience have *its* perfect work, that you may be perfect and complete, lacking nothing. If any of you lacks wisdom, let him ask of God, who gives liberally and without reproach, and it will be given to him. But let him ask in faith, with no doubting, for he who doubts is like a wave of the sea driven and tossed by the wind." (James 1:2-6)

The reward for the testing of faith is patience, which benefits us in all aspects of life, as it ultimately perfects and matures us. It is also the way to receive wisdom, which we can have infinite amounts of, as God always gives it to us when we ask in faith.

Faith results in action and action is required to demonstrate faith.

What *does it* profit, my brethren, if someone says he has faith but does not have works? Can faith save him? If a brother or sister is naked and destitute of daily food, and one of you says to them, "Depart in peace, be warmed and filled," but you do not give them the things which are needed for the body, what *does it* profit? Thus also, faith by itself, if it does not have works, is dead. But someone will say, "You have faith, and I have works." Show me your faith without your works, and I will show you my faith by my works. You believe that there is one God. You do well. Even the demons believe—and tremble! But do you want to know, O foolish man, that faith without works is dead? Was not Abraham our father justified by works when he offered Isaac his son on the altar?

Do you see that faith was working together with his works, and by works, faith was made perfect? And the Scripture was fulfilled which says, "Abraham believed God, and it was accounted to him for righteousness." And he was called the friend of God. You see then that a man is justified by works, and not by faith only. Likewise, was not Rahab the harlot also justified by works when she received the messengers and sent *them* out another way? For as the body without the spirit is dead, so faith without works is dead also." (James 2:14-26)

Faith brings us closer to God.

"Let us draw near with a true heart in full assurance of faith, having our hearts sprinkled from an evil conscience and our bodies washed with pure water. Let us hold fast the confession of *our* hope without wavering, for He who promised *is* faithful." (Hebrews 10:22-23)

Justification:

Justification means to be made righteous. We are made righteous because of Jesus and His finished work, and we receive that through faith.

The just shall live by faith.

"Now the just shall live by faith; but if anyone draws back, my soul has no pleasure in him" (Hebrews 10:38)

"For in it, the righteousness of God is revealed from faith to faith; as it is written, 'The just shall live by faith.'" (Romans 1:17)

"But that no one is justified (declared righteous) by the law in the sign of God is evident, for 'the just shall live by faith.'" (Galatians 3:11)

These three verses are referencing the Prophet Habakkuk's question of justice to the Lord, who answered him:

"Behold the proud, his soul is not upright in him; but the just shall live by faith." (Habakkuk 2:4)

Furthermore, we cannot obtain Christ's righteousness without faith and trying to gain it any other way is wrong, especially by trying to do it solely through our own works.

"Know that a person is not justified by the works of the law but by faith in Jesus Christ. So, we, too, have put our faith in Christ Jesus that we may be justified by faith in Christ and not by the works of the law because, by the works of the law, no one will be justified." (Galatians 2:16)

"You have become estranged from Christ, you who attempt to be justified by law; you have fallen from grace. For we, through the Spirit, eagerly wait for the hope of righteousness by faith." (Galatians 5:4-5)

"I have fought the good fight, I have finished the race, I have kept the faith. Now there is in store for me the crown of righteousness, which the Lord, the righteous Judge, will award to me on that day – and not only to me but also to all who have longed for His appearing." (2 Timothy 4:7-8

Faith and Joy:

"Though you have not seen Him, you love Him, and even though you do not see Him now, you believe in Him and are filled with inexpressible and glorious joy, for you are receiving the end result of your faith, the salvation of your souls." (1 Peter 1:8-9)

It is here we see that one gift leads to another! Salvation is connected to faith, which is connected to joy! When the Father sees our faith and our unconditional trust in Him like a child with a parent, He delights in giving us joy. This is not just the happiness that the world gives at times and can come and go, but a deep joy in the core of our hearts that is always present and cultivated by His guidance and wisdom throughout the course of our lives. Our increased faith leads to increased joy, which then increases our faith and so forth. If you wish to begin the voyage of faith and joy, now is the time to ask Jesus!

Prayer:

Jesus, You said that we will receive anything we ask for in prayer if we have faith. Just like the Apostles, I am asking You for more faith. Thank You for this gift of faith You have already so freely given, and thank You for multiplying it. I want to live my life according to faith, and wherever it may be lacking, please fill in the gap as I grow. Thank you, Lord. In Jesus' name, amen.

"Whatever you ask in prayer, you will receive if you have faith." (Matthew 21:22)

And the Apostles said to the Lord, "Increase our faith!" (Luke 17:5)

Chapter 3

Joy

Oh, thank God for the gift of joy! Through this comes a deeper sense of gladness and delight. Joy is lasting, satisfying, and ever-present. It comes from the spirit of the Lord who lives in us. This joy does not equate to ordinary happiness, which is fickle. Joy is independent of circumstances, and that's great news! This means that no matter what we are going through, we can always have and ask for more joy. The world and the people in it are always searching or longing for true joy and yet can never quite seem to find it. It is not of this world nor attainable apart from a true relationship with the Lord. When we ask Jesus into our hearts and begin our lives of faith in Him, we are given joy abundantly and eternally. Although life might still have ups and downs and trials may come, we can always count on that deep joy in our hearts and spirits that only comes from the Father!

"Ask and you will receive, that your joy may be full." (John 16:24)

God loves to fill us with joy! As we spend time abiding in Him, we receive it more and more! He is our ever help and our joy. Apart from Him we are truly lost and empty.

In God's presence, there is joy.

"You make known to me the path of life; in your presence, there is fullness of joy; at your right hand are pleasures forevermore." (Psalm 16:11)

We enter God's presence through ways like reading the word, praying, fasting, worshipping, and fellowship with other believers. There is always an abundance of His presence available, but sometimes, we must quiet the noise around us and focus on Him. Turning our attention to God requires humbling ourselves and results in a great spiritual reward.

"He must increase, but I *must* decrease." (John 3:30)

In doing so, we receive the fullness of joy, as mentioned above in Psalm 16. The more of Him, the more joy!

We get to celebrate Joy!

"There, I will go to the altar of God, to God – the source of all my joy. I will praise you with my harp, O God, my God!" (Psalm 43:4)

Other translations of this verse say that God is our exceeding and greatest joy! It's perhaps the most fun gift of all. After all, who doesn't love joy? I certainly love it! Even if we are in a rough season that is meant to push or challenge us, we can still walk through it joyfully. I think this is a point Christians often miss – they think they must suffer at times, more frequently than times of celebrating. While that's true, we have intentional sufferings that are temporary and purposeful, and we can simultaneously live through them with joy. A great example of this is Paul's writings in the book of Philippians. It is considered the most joyful book in the Bible, although it was written in prison. Another example is the Psalms, many of which express deep longing but are always followed by ones with themes of celebration and joy.

King David, who wrote most of the Psalms, had extreme emotional highs and lows but was considered a man after God's own heart because he always came back to joy! He exemplifies the heart of a true worshipper, always being grateful while still sitting in the ebbs and flows of raw emotions.

"My lips will shout for joy, when I sign praises to you; my soul also, which you have redeemed." (Psalm 71:23)

"But let all who take refuge in you rejoice; let them sing joyful praises forever. Spread your protection over them, that all who love your name may be filled with joy." (Psalm 5:11)

It isn't just a gift; it is also an instruction.

Rejoicing is a constant choice we make. In a split moment, we can decide to turn our attitude in a positive direction. When we rejoice in the Lord always and through all circumstances, we escape the traps of this world that are designed to rob us of our joy and happiness. God does not instruct us to put on a fake smile or pretend that we are just happy on a worldly level but to maintain that deep joy that He has gifted us. This world might try to break us down and try to fill us with negativity, but thankfully we serve a God who encourages us to keep that joy no matter what as He fills our hearts day by day and moment by moment!

"Rejoice in the Lord always, again I will say, rejoice." (Philippians 4:4)

"Clap your hands, all you nations; shout to God with cries of joy." (Psalm 47:1)

"Rejoice always, pray without ceasing, in everything give thanks; for this is the will of God in Christ Jesus for you." (1 Thessalonians 5:16-18)

"So, rejoice in the LORD and be glad, all you who obey Him! Shout for joy, all you whose hearts are pure." (Psalm 32:11)

"The Lord has done it in this very day; let us rejoice today and be glad." (Psalm 118:24)

Sometimes, that decision is to be made, although it may be difficult. Living a joyful life does not mean focusing on controlling outcomes but rather being content regardless. If life isn't currently going the way we would like, we can still choose joy and reap the benefits of doing so.

"Though the fig tree does not bud and there are no grapes on the vines, though the olive crop fails and the fields produce to food, though there are no sheep in the pen and no cattle in the stalls, yet I will rejoice in the Lord, I will be joyful in God my Savior." (Habakkuk 3:17-18)

"You have put more joy in my heart than they have when their grain and wine abound." (Psalm 4:7)

God will help us:

Joy is another one of His gifts to us as believers and He consoles and speaks to us to restore and fill our joy in Him.

"When anxiety was great within me, your consolation brought me joy." (Psalm 94:19)

"These things I have spoken to you, that my joy may be in you, and that your joy may be full." (John 15:11)

The joy of the Lord gives glory to God. Our example of living in joy can be one of the greatest witnesses to unbelievers. They will notice that we have something different inside of us, this desirable quality. When others ask us how we can be so joyful, even while having less materially than them, we can give all the praise and honor to God. This type of joy and gratitude brings freedom and encourages salvation as well as spiritual discipline.

Prayer:

Thank you, Jesus, for your gift of joy. Whether I'm on a mountain-top or in a valley, I will choose to be joyful. I know joy does not depend on my circumstances, and for that, I am grateful. You give not as the world gives but so much better. I am so glad I can live a lifestyle of joy! Thank you, Lord, so much; you are so, so good! In Jesus' name, amen.

"Give thanks to the Lord, for He is good!" (Psalm 118:1)

Chapter 4

Peace

Peace is another gift from God that He has generously given to us through Jesus. This peace is always available in every situation. It is greater than anything material that the world has to offer.

"Now, may the Lord of peace Himself give you peace at all times and in every way. The Lord be with all of you." (2 Thessalonians 3:16)

"Peace, I leave you, My peace I give you; not as the world gives, do I give to you. Do not let your hearts be troubled, nor fearful." (John 14:27)

How to gain God's peace:

"Don't worry about anything; instead, pray about everything. Tell God what you need, and thank Him for all He has done. Then, you will experience God's peace, which exceeds anything we can understand. His peace will guard your hearts and minds as you live in Christ Jesus." (Philippians 4:6-7)

"Finally, brothers and sisters, whatever is true, whatever is noble, whatever is right, whatever is pure, whatever is lovely, whatever is admirable – if anything is excellent or praiseworthy – think about such things. Whatever you have learned or received or heard from me, or seen in me – put into practice. And the peace of God will be with you." (Philippians 4:8-9)

The Apostle Paul wrote step-by-step instructions on how to receive God's peace. He first says not to be anxious but to make our requests known to God and be thankful upon reflecting on all He has already done. Regardless of our situation, His peace will surpass it as we live in Him. Paul goes on to say that we should really focus on all the positives and follow the examples he has shown. Focusing on positive affirmations is not some "secret." In fact, a lot of New Age false teachings were stolen and twisted from this verse. The main important component was eliminated.

That is the power of Christ Jesus. Anytime something is taken from the source while removing the very thing that makes it true, it is not only misleading but also dangerously deceiving. We can discern what is or is not truth is by testing the idea through scripture and seeing how it aligns. Jesus is the way and the truth, and therefore, the way to truth will always point to Him.

When we need more peace, we can always ask God!

"For God is not the author of confusion but of peace, as in all the churches of the saints." (1 Corinthians 14:33)

"I have told you these things so that in Me you may have peace. In this world, you will have trouble. But take heart! I have overcome the world." (John 13:33)

We need His peace! His word explicitly states that we will have challenges in life. God never promised us an easy life, but He did promise that He will be with us, and give us everything we need to overcome our troubles. His peace, joy, hope, love, and strength are with us.

Unfortunately, much of the modern church preaches "feel good" messages that make new believers feel like God is not with them if something is going wrong. However, a basic study of scripture proves that we don't enter into this so-called "perfect" life when we accept Jesus into our hearts. The thought that God will magically pay all bills, take away all physical and emotional pain, make everyone like you and be nice to you, and so forth, is false. Although He does do miracles all the time, and He is a provider and healer, He is not some magic wand to wave around, so we have our way. He is most interested in making us more like Him. If we had our way all the time, it would certainly lead to damage and destruction as we are flawed and limited in our scope.

He sees and knows all. He knows that granting us peace in a storm before calming the storm will be more sufficient and life giving to our souls. When we receive the peace He so freely gives, we learn to become more like Him and closer to Him. Our dependence relies on Him, so we are assured that life in Him is greater than without. He will never give us a life where we think we don't need Him and that's amazing! Having Him is the reward and the abundant life.

To receive and maintain peace, there are some conditions:

"Abstain from every form of evil. Now may the God of peace Himself sanctify you completely; and may your whole spirit, soul, and body be preserved blameless at the coming of our Lord Jesus Christ. He who calls you is faithful, who also will do it." (1 Thessalonians 5:22-24)

We can't be at peace while living in sin. Oftentimes, Christians wonder why they don't "feel peace" about a specific situation or relationship, but what they fail to do is look inward and ask themselves if they are being obedient to God. Sometimes, God doesn't give peace in a certain area of our lives because He is trying to call us out of it.

Another important aspect to note is that peace is not a feeling. It is not an emotion. It is a spiritual gift that affects our body, mind, and soul. We can have peace while in a storm or when surrounded by external chaos. We can have peace while simultaneously grieving. There is no limit to peace, and we must be cautious while chasing a mere feeling of peace because our hearts can be deceitful and play tricks on us.

Prayer:

Dear God, I come before You asking for Your peace over my situation and over my life. I need You every single day. Although I may be in a storm, I have full faith and confidence that Your peace will sustain me and comfort me. Thank you, Jesus, for this gift. I will continue to pray about everything and give You thanks! I will keep my mind on You. You guard my heart and dwell within me. Thank you! In Jesus' name, I pray, amen.

Chapter 5

Hope

"This *hope* we have as an anchor to the soul, both sure and steadfast, and which enters the *Presence* behind the veil." (Hebrews 6:19)

Hope is an anchor to the soul in which we enter the Presence of the Lord. The term veil also translates to curtain, which refers to what is at the entrance of the most Holy Place in the Tabernacle, the temple of God. Before we had Jesus, who tore this veil once and for all, only the high priests could enter this physical place to worship and commune with God. Jesus became our ultimate High Priest, and through this hope we have in Him, we, too, can have access to the Father. It is no longer limited to those who have been deemed worthy by priesthood but is now available to all ordinary people as well.

Hope is produced by joy and peace.

"May the God of hope fill you with all joy and peace as you trust in Him, so that you may overflow with hope by the power of the Holy Spirit." (Romans 15:13)

In the previous chapters, we highlighted the gifts of joy and peace, and naturally, those lead to this gift of hope! God is a God of hope, and when we walk in alignment with Him, receiving the abundant life He has given us on earth and in eternity, His hope is ours too!

He gives us hope.

"For I know the plans I have for you, declares the Lord, plans to prosper you and not to harm you. Plans to give you hope and a future." (Jeremiah 29:11)

Not only does He know the plans He has for us to give us hope, but also, He actually knew those plans before we were even born. His plans have always been to give us hope.

"Before I formed you in the womb, I knew you." (Jeremiah 1:5)

A lack of hope.

"Hope deferred makes the heart sick, But *when* the desire comes, *it is* a tree of life." (Proverbs 13:12)

"The hope of the righteous shall be gladness: but the expectation of the wicked shall perish." (Proverbs 10:28)

Life without hope is, well, hopeless. It is no life at all. The Bible teaches us how important it is to be filled with hope, and this hope points us to the *fact* that God's desires will come to pass. He is the very One who puts His desires in our hearts. Therefore, we can grasp the true hope He gives and know that it isn't delusional thinking but rather extremely tangible and realistic. Our hopeful expectations in Him are vital to our well-being.

Yet, sometimes, we must force it.

It is necessary to note that although it is not God's plan for us, we can be without hope. This is when we are faced with the choice to choose it.

"Rejoice in hope, be patient in tribulations, be constant in prayer." (Romans 12:12)

"But as for me, I watch in hope for the LORD, I wait for God my Savior; my God will hear me." (Micah 7:7)

Holding onto hope isn't always our first human reaction. It can be easy to fall into discouragement or distraction. We have the ability to decide if we want to cling to hope or go about our days hopeless, which in turn is so much worse. So why would anyone want to do that? Next time you are faced with a decision to remain hopeful or give up, it's clearly better to choose hope!

Hope and Salvation.

"For we were saved in this hope, but hope that is seen is not hope; for why does one still hope for what he sees? But if we hope for what we do not see, we eagerly wait for it with perseverance." (Romans 8:24-25)

"Blessed be the God and Father of our Lord Jesus Christ! According to His great mercy, He has caused us to be born again to a living hope through the resurrection of Jesus Christ from the dead." (1 Peter 1:3)

Prayer:

Dear God, I come before You today so grateful for the hope You have given me! Help me always remain focused on You and stay hopeful. I know Your will for my life will come to pass, and it will be better than I could have ever expected or imagined on my own. I know You are working all things together for my good and Your glory. You already have plans for my future. I can receive your gift of hope because You are the God of hope! I look forward to all You have for me in this life and in Heaven. Thank you Lord! In Jesus' mighty name, amen.

44

Chapter 6

Love

"Let all that you do be done with love." (1 Corinthians 16:14)

"Love is patient and kind; love does not envy or boast; it is not arrogant or rude. It does not insist on its own way; it is not irritable or resentful; it does not rejoice at wrongdoing but rejoices with the truth. Love bears all things, believes all things, hopes all things, endures all things." (1 Corinthians 13:4-7)

"And above all these put on love, which binds everything together in perfect harmony." (Colossians 3:14)

"So now faith, hope, and love abide, these three, but the greatest of these is love." (1 Corinthians 13:13)

"Greater love has no one than this, than to lay down one's life for his friends." (John 15:13)

"For God so loved the world that He gave His only begotten Son, that whoever believes in Him should not perish but have everlasting life." (John 3:16)

"Dear friends, let us love one another, for love comes from God. Everyone who loves has been born of God and knows God. Whoever does not love does not know God, because God is love. This is how God showed love among us: He sent His one and only Son into the world that we might live through Him. This is love: not that we loved God, but that He loved us and sent His Son as an atoning sacrifice for our sins. Dear friends, since God so loved us, we also ought to love one another." (1 John 4:7-11)

"Above all, love each other deeply, because love covers over a multitude of sins." (1 Peter 4:8)

"Husbands, love your wives, as Christ loved the church and gave Himself up for her." (Ephesians 5:25)

"Always be humble and gentle. Be patient with each other, making allowance for each other's faults because of your love." (Ephesians 4:2)

These verses state bluntly that we must love one another, despite their earnings (or lack thereof) of it, just as God loves us. We are to be like Him in all we do. Jesus even talks about the importance of love as the most important of all commands, and even states that if we love Him, we must love others too. In the Gospel of Matthew, one of the religious leaders, who was an expert in the Old Testament Law, tried to test Jesus by asking Him:

"Teacher, which is the greatest commandment in the Law?" Jesus replied: "Love your Lord your God with all your heart and with all your soul and with all your mind." (Matthew 22:36-37)

Here, Jesus directly quoted the writings of Moses in the Torah.

"You shall love the LORD your God with all your heart and with all your soul and with all your might." (Deuteronomy 6:5)

The later written Hebrew scriptures further confirm this verse throughout the Old Testament. In reference to King Josiah:

"Before him, there was no king like him who turned to the LORD with all his heart, soul, and might, according to all the Law of Moses, nor did any like him arise after him." (2 Kings 23:25)

This law is also repeated in the New Testament Gospels, as seen in Mark 12:30 and Luke 10:27. When the Bible repeats information or words, it multiplies its significance. Jesus goes on to say not only must we love Him, but it is, first and foremost, the most important commandment of all.

"This is the first and greatest commandment. And the second is like it: 'Love your neighbor as yourself.' All the Law and the Prophets hang on these two commandments." (Matthew 22:38-40)

Jesus again quoted the Law. These words were spoken to Moses by the Father.

"Do not seek revenge or bear a grudge against anyone among your people, but love your neighbor as yourself. I am the LORD." (Leviticus 19:18)

From this passage in Matthew and the scriptures that Jesus quoted, we can see that loving God and loving our neighbor are the greatest commandments. We can also see that the Law is important to obey. Jesus states explicitly:

"If you love me, you will keep my commandments." (John 14:15)

We know that these commandments still apply because:

"Jesus Christ *is* the same yesterday, today, and forever." (Hebrews 13:8)

"God is not a man that He should lie" (Numbers 23:19)

He doesn't change. He gave us these commandments and the entirety of the Law because He loves us so much. He fulfilled all 613 commandments in the Old Testament, which no human has or ever will do because we are imperfect. He loves us so much that He came to be that perfect example, and to live the Law so that we, through Him, can receive the blessings of the Law. Our part is to honor Him by obedience to His word.

"Do not think that I have come to abolish the Law or the Prophets; I have not come to abolish them but to fulfill them. For truly I tell you, until Heaven and earth disappear, not the smallest letter, not the least stroke of a pen, will by any means disappear from the Law until everything is accomplished. Therefore, anyone who sets aside one of the least of these commands and teaches others accordingly will be called least in the kingdom of Heaven, but whoever practices and teaches these commands will be called great in the kingdom of Heaven. For I tell you that unless your righteousness surpasses that of the Pharisees and the teachers of the law, you will certainly not enter the kingdom of Heaven." (Matthew 5:17-20)

Thank you, Jesus, for fulfilling the Law so that in you, we may enter the kingdom of Heaven!

Love is a gift.

Love is definitely one of the greatest gifts that God can give us. Everyone is searching for love in some form, and it has inspired humans since the very beginning. People are all longing for unconditional love, and yet God is the only source where this can be found. Unlike human love, which can be conditional or fleeting if it isn't real, God's love has no end and no other condition than loving Him and trusting in Him alone. We love because He first loved us.

Jesus is the greatest love there is.

Jesus was the ultimate expression of God's love for us when He died on the cross for our sins. Even though we did not know the Lord or love Him yet, God still loved us as sinners and gave us a way out through His only begotten Son. The sacrifice of Jesus and His forgiveness of our sins is a type of love that we can always count on and know that it is unconditional. Even though many of us have been hurt by human love in some way over the years, we have a source of never-ending true love through the Father.

No other love can compare!

When we find that love in Christ and He comes into our hearts, all other forms of love can never compare. God can and will still bless His children with the romantic love of a spouse or the deep love of children and so forth, but every earthly love is but a shadow of that true unconditional eternal love that God has for us and gives us freely through His Son. Once we have tasted that love from Heaven, we can rest assured that we will be filled in our hearts forever.

"Taste and see that the Lord is good." (Psalm 34:8)

Prayer:

Lord, help me to accept the immeasurable love you have for me. It's far beyond what I can ever begin to fathom. Although at times I feel so unlovable, your word is truth, and nothing can separate me from your love. Help me to rest in this truth so that I can love you and love others well, just as you've commanded. Thank you, Father, for embodying love and that love living in me. I am committed to becoming complete in you and being more loving. I repent of all the times I have made choices and actions that were not out of a place of love. I restart now and will let all I do be done in love because of your great love for me. I pray this in Jesus' name, amen.

Chapter 7

Sound Mind

A gift we tend to overlook is that of a sound mind. A sound mind is a freedom from fear, indecisiveness, confusion, and anxiety. Many have grown so comfortable in their minds that they don't realize we have a gift available to us, which is far better.

"For God has not given us a spirit of fear, but of power, love, and of a sound mind." (2 Timothy 1:7)

If we are feeling clouded, unsure, or stifled in decision-making, those are good indicators that there is an attack on our minds. As believers, that is not our portion.

We can turn our hearts and minds to God, and He will give us the clarity and comfort of a sound mind. We can live in mental freedom.

Anxiety happens.

We know how prevalent anxiety is in today's world. Yet, it's not a new condition! It is actually a weapon of the enemy to paralyze us. We have often searched in the wrong places to calm the effects of these mental attacks. We have tried to manage them solely through self-control, reliant upon our own strength. When that hasn't worked, we have tried to escape them through external sources. Worse then, we have even resulted to numbing them through any means we find necessary. Billion-dollar pharmaceutical companies offer a false promise that they have a miracle solution. That, in most instances, has left us feeling worse than before. The great news is that we don't have to turn to modern medical developments to cure them (I'm not a Doctor, so don't sue me!). What I am saying is that, biblically, a sound mind is the antidote to anxiety, and it is freely available without negative side effects.

God doesn't want us to live in constant anxiety.

People will spend a fortune on various ways to calm their minds and deal with the fears and anxieties that this world bombards us with daily. From seeking out healthy forms of therapy to illegal and destructive drugs, the average person is living in a world now where fear and panic seem to be everywhere. There always seems to be something new to worry about, and the news is always filled with some new fear or terror to rob you of peace of mind and contentment with life. However, God does not desire us to live this way, and He has given us both the chance to live with peace of mind and also the way to find that through Him. Reading His word reminds us of the promises He has for us. This promise is the spirit of power, love, and a sound mind. This is the Holy Spirit working inside of our innermost beings. God tells us step by step how to activate the Holy Spirit's work within us:

"Seek first the kingdom of God and His righteousness, and all these things will be added unto you. Therefore, do not be anxious about tomorrow, for tomorrow will be anxious for itself. Sufficient for the day is its own trouble." (Matthew 6:33-34)

"Do not be anxious about anything, but in every situation, by prayer and petition, with thanksgiving, let your requests be made known to God. And the peace of God, which surpasses all understanding, will guard your hearts and minds in Christ Jesus." (Philippians 4:6-7)

"Therefore, humble yourselves under the mighty hand of God so that He may exalt you at the proper time, having cast all your anxiety on Him because He cares for you." (1 Peter 5:6-7)

His word shows us practical tools to release anxiety. We seek Him first, pray, and humble ourselves. The answer is very simple, with clear direction.

Having a truly sound mind.

Now, some anxiety is obviously a part of life, and living with your head in the clouds and denying that there is anything scary in this world is not a healthy way to live either. However, there is a difference between running from the anxieties of life and giving them over to the Lord so that He can take that burden and carry you through this anxious and tumultuous world. Having a sound mind means accepting that life will sometimes bring different stressors and issues, but we can rest assured that the God who created all things can get us through anything, and He will use all circumstances for good in the end. In an anxious world of unknown fears, what a blessing it is to have a known God who wants nothing more than to let us live happy and healthy lives without enslavement to fear or worry!

Verses against fear:

We must be diligent while seeking a sound mind. There is full opposition against us. In fact, the world we inhabit seems to thrive on fear and worry. We have an unseen enemy in this world who wants nothing more than to rob all people of their hope, joy, peace, and love. Seeking a sound mind is not just to live in a dreamy state with no concerns for what is happening in reality. It is to allow the peace that God has to offer to rule over your mind so that you might be able to withstand the evil in this world that tries so hard to keep you anxious and depressed when God wants nothing but the opposite for you in your life!

"Be sober-minded; be watchful. Your adversary, the devil, prowls around like a roaring lion, seeking someone to devour." (1 Peter 5:8)

We don't have to be on guard alone; God will help us! As we partner with Him, He works His power through us. How awesome is it that we have the winner on our side?

"I will instruct you and teach you in the way you should go; I will advise you with My eye upon you." (Psalm 32:8)

Then Jesus spoke to them again, saying, "I am the light of the world. He who follows Me will not walk in the darkness, but will have the Light of life." (John 8:12)

He instructs, teaches, and advises us. He leads us on the right path. He is so near us, guiding the way.

Following God

Following God means saying no to ungodly things. If we want His gifts, we must also turn from what is not of Him.

"For where envy and self-seeking *exist,* confusion and every evil thing *are* there." (James 3:16)

If we fall back into our own ways or rely on ourselves, we are rejecting God's gift of a sound mind. It is important to no longer agree with old mindsets. We are new creations in Christ.

This means that anyone who belongs to Christ has become a new person. "The old life is gone; a new life has begun!" (2 Corinthians 5:17)

Prayer:

Lord Jesus, thank You for the peace and sound mind that you have to offer in this anxious world. Thank you for making me brand new! Please keep me focused on You and allow your peace to rule my mind in all things. I lift up my worries and fears before You and trust that You will take care of them and use all things for good. Thank you, Jesus, for a sound mind and clarity in all circumstances. Amen!

Chapter 8

Healing

"For I *am* the LORD who heals you." (Exodus 15:26)

Healing is for everyone.

One of the most common issues in this life is that we all need healing in some way. Everyone, on some level, has wounds that need to be addressed and fully healed in life. Some people have mild wounds, and some people have very severe wounds, but each of us is blessed to have a great healer that we can approach through prayer any moment that we wish.

"LORD my God, I called to you for help, and you healed me." (Psalm 30:2)

When we call out to God, He hears us, listens to us, and answers.

"He sent out His word and healed them; He rescued them from the grave." (Psalm 107:19-20)

"And the prayer offered in faith will make the sick person well; the Lord will raise them up." (James 5:14-15)

We have a direct speed dial (wow, I just aged myself) line to the Healer. We can call Him at any time, and He will pick up.

Jesus isn't just some mystical healer; He is the Great Physician who can and will heal wounds at the core that we might not even realize we have. These wounds may go deeper than we realize. We might think we have a mere physical ailment or emotional pain, but often times, there is an underlying spiritual connection to what we see on the surface. We don't always just need our symptoms to be relieved, but we need healing at the root so the illness never returns. Thank God, He has given us these gifts of physical, emotional, and spiritual healing!

King Hezekiah

The story of Hezekiah's healing is so interesting. It shows us that not only He does heal us, but He speaks to us and allows us to have a part in our own destiny, through our relationship with Him.

"About that time, Hezekiah became deathly ill, and the Prophet Isaiah, son of Amoz, went to visit him. He gave the king this message: "This is what the LORD says: Set your affairs in order, for you are going to die. You will not recover from this illness." When Hezekiah heard this, he turned his face to the wall and prayed to the LORD, "Remember, O LORD, how I have always been faithful to you and have served you single-mindedly, always doing what pleases you." Then he broke down and wept bitterly. But before Isaiah left the middle courtyard, the message came to him from the LORD: "Go back to Hezekiah, the leader of my people. Tell him, 'This is what the LORD, the God of your ancestor David, says: I have heard your prayer and seen your tears. I will heal you, and three days from now, you will get out of bed and go to the Temple of the LORD.

I will add fifteen years to your life, and I will rescue you and this city from the king of Assyria. I will defend this city for my own honor and the sake of my servant David." Then Isaiah said, "Make an ointment from figs." So, Hezekiah's servants spread the ointment over the boil, and Hezekiah recovered! Meanwhile, Hezekiah had said to Isaiah, "What sign will the LORD give to prove that he will heal me and that I will go to the Temple of the LORD three days from now?" Isaiah replied, "This is the sign from the LORD to prove that He will do as He promised. Would you like the shadow on the sundial to go forward ten steps or backward ten steps?" "The shadow always moves forward," Hezekiah replied, "so that would be easy. Make it go ten steps backward instead." So, Isaiah the Prophet asked the LORD to do this, and He caused the shadow to move ten steps backward on the sundial of Ahaz!" (2 Kings 20:1-10)

God specifically answered King Hezekiah's prayers. He heard his cries and promised healing. In addition to healing him, He proved it to him through signs. This is confirmation that the Lord cares so much about us, and He loves to communicate with us. He invites us to have a conversation with Him!

Physical Healing

"The LORD sustains them on their sickbed and restores them from their bed of illness." (Psalm 41:3)

"I will restore you to health and heal your wounds," declares the LORD. (Jeremiah 30:17)

God's intention is to heal all. We see this in the example that Jesus lived.

"Jesus went through all the towns and villages, teaching in their synagogues, proclaiming the good news of the kingdom, and healing every disease and sickness." (Matthew 9:35)

And He said to her, "Daughter, your faith has made you well; go in peace, and be healed of your disease." (Mark 5:34)

"Jesus went from there and came to the Sea of Galilee. Then He went up the mountain and sat down. Many people came to Him. They brought with them those who were not able to walk. They brought those who were not able to see. They brought those who were not able to hear or speak and many others. Then, they put them at the feet of Jesus, and He healed them. All the people wondered. They saw how those who could not walk were now walking.

They saw how those who could not see were now seeing, and they gave thanks to the God of the Jews." (Matthew 15:29-31)

"And When Jesus entered Peter's house, He saw his mother-in-law lying sick with a fever. He touched her hand, and the fever left her, and she rose and began to serve Him. That evening, they brought to Him many who were oppressed by demons, and He cast out the spirits with a word and healed all who were sick." (Matthew 8:14-16)

Even when you're ill, God is still in control!

When we come to God, we might come with all sorts of illnesses that rob our hope and joy and make it seem as if there is no chance of happiness in our lives.

"Have mercy on me, LORD, for I am faint; heal me LORD, for my bones are in agony." (Psalm 6:2)

Although God can obviously do whatever He wishes, many times, He gives people certain issues to face physically because it is part of their testimony, and He will use it for good in the end. Human logic might tell us that being sick or being born with some health issue is a reason to give up and live in despair, but God loves to take circumstances that the world sees as hopeless and use them to bless someone and glorify Himself in the end, too! God might do miraculous healings as He has done in the Bible, and still does all the time, but even more important is that He might use a negative circumstance for a positive outcome in ways that we could never imagine.

"And we know that all things work together for good to those who love God, to those who are called according to *His* purpose." (Romans 8:28)

Emotional Healing.

"He heals the brokenhearted and binds up their wounds." (Psalm 147:3)

Emotional wounds can be just as destructive and painful as physical wounds, and, many times, they can be much more severe. There is no wound too deep that the Great Physician cannot heal. Just as with physical illness or sickness, God can and often does use emotional injuries to create stronger and more resilient people for His kingdom who can testify that they overcame anything through Christ, who gave them strength. If you are suffering right now and it makes no sense, don't give up hope! God might not just heal you but also surprise you with how much He uses you in powerful ways to leave a positive impact in this world that you can barely imagine. He cares so deeply for those who are hurting.

"'He will wipe away every tear from their eyes. There will be no more death' or mourning or crying or pain, for the old order of things has passed away." (Revelation 21:4)

"The righteous cry out, and the LORD hears them; He delivers them from all their troubles. The LORD is close to the brokenhearted and saves those who are crushed in spirit." (Psalm 34:17-18)

"I have seen their ways, but I will heal them; I will guide them and restore comfort to Israel's mourners, creating praise on their lips. Peace, peace, to those far and near," says the LORD. "And I will heal them." (Isaiah 57:18-19)

Spiritual Healing.

"Beloved, I pray in every way you may succeed *and* prosper and be in good health [physically], just as [I know] your soul prospers [spiritually]." (3 John 1:2)

Many people have been hurt by churches and people claiming to be believers in Jesus. If someone asked your average atheist what their background was, it would probably be surprising to find out just how many of them came from a Christian upbringing and experienced something negative that impacted their faith and spiritual life drastically. Many people running from God or rejecting God have just been pushed away by bad examples or circumstances that did not show them an accurate depiction of who Jesus really is and how He can bless their lives and fulfill them at the deepest level.

Spiritual healing is one of God's greatest miracles that He can do for people, taking their negative experiences and turning them into a truly powerful testimony in the future. Sometimes, God allows people to go through these experiences so that they will have a genuine heart of love and understanding for others who have gone through similar wounds that misrepresented what faith should be. If you have deep hurts from past churches or Christians, know that Christ cares very deeply about this, and He will reveal Himself in a way that will go beyond anything imaginable! When it comes to healing the wounds of the spirit, never forget that our Great Physician is a master surgeon whose love can cleanse even the deepest of wounds in our hearts and souls.

"Come to me, all you who are weary and burdened, and I will give you rest. Take my yoke upon you and learn from me, for I am gentle and humble in heart, and you will find rest for your souls. For my yoke is easy and my burden is light." (Matthew 11:28-30)

"Surely, He took up our pain and bore our suffering, yet we considered Him punished by God, stricken by Him, and afflicted. But He was pierced for our transgressions, He was crushed for our iniquities; the punishment that brought us peace was on Him, and by His wounds we are healed." (Isaiah 53:4-5)

Even those who have hurt us are loved by God and are healed through Him. Isaiah foretold the coming Messiah, Jesus, who would later come to walk this earth and bring us ultimate healing. Whoever loves God and comes to Him will receive spiritual healing for eternity.

"Because he loves me," says the LORD, "I will rescue him; I will protect him, for he acknowledges my name. He will call on me, and I will answer him; I will be with him in trouble, I will deliver him and honor him. With long life, I will satisfy him and show him my salvation." (Psalm 91:14-16)

Laying of hands

Laying of the hands is one of the ways Jesus healed, and He gives us that spiritual gift to do ourselves.

"And He took them in His arms and blessed them, laying His hands on them." (Mark 10:16)

"And when He had called His twelve disciples to *Him*, He gave them power *over* unclean spirits, to cast them out, and to heal all kinds of sickness and all kinds of disease." (Matthew 10:1)

"It happened that the father of Publius lay sick with fever and dysentery. And Paul visited him and prayed, and putting his hands on him, healed him." (Acts 28:8)

"Now, when the sun was setting, all those who had any who were sick with various diseases brought them to Him, and He laid His hands on every one of them and healed them. And demons also came out of many, crying, "You are the Son of God!" But He rebuked them and would not allow them to speak, because they knew that He was the Christ." (Luke 4:40-41)

The laying of the hands has the power to heal all types of sickness. Whether it be physical, emotional or spiritual, the gift of healing works in and through us. The

Apostle Paul writes about spiritual gifts in his first letter to the church of Corinth.

"There are diversities of gifts, but the same Spirit. There are differences of ministries, but the same Lord. And there are diversities of activities, but it is the same God who works all in all. But the manifestation of the Spirit is given to each one for the profit of *all:* for to one is given the word of wisdom through the Spirit, to another the word of knowledge through the same Spirit, to another faith by the same Spirit, to another gifts of healings by the same Spirit, to another the working of miracles, to another prophecy, to another discerning of spirits, to another *different* kinds of tongues, to another the interpretation of tongues. But one and the same Spirit works all these things, distributing to each one individually as He wills." (1 Corinthians 12:1-11)

We see here that we are all given gifts of the Holy Spirit. We all, as believers and followers of Jesus, have the same Spirit living inside us. Although some are given specific gifts in greater measure, we all have the ability to lay hands on the sick and pray for them to be healed.

"Is anyone among you sick? Let him call for the elders of the church, and let them pray over him, anointing him with oil in the name of the Lord. And the prayer of faith will save the one who is sick, and the Lord will raise him up.

And if he has committed sins, he will be forgiven. Therefore, confess your sins to one another and pray for one another, that you may be healed. The prayer of a righteous person has great power as it is working." (James 5:14-16)

Notice this passage speaks to calling on the elders of the church and using anointing oil as they pray for healing. This may suggest that as we grow higher in the ways of the Lord, in spiritual maturity, our gifts of healing may increase and be more effective. Jesus stated that prayers while fasting will have a greater impact.

"But this kind of demon does not go out but by prayer and by going without good so you can pray better." (Matthew 17:21)

Perhaps the elders of the church of which James spoke were disciplined in this area of prayers and fasting. Nevertheless, we can be assured that as we are submitted to the Spirit of the Lord, by decreasing the desires of our flesh, He can work true wonders through us.

"He must increase, but I *must* decrease." (John 3:30)

Forgiveness

An exponential way to increase the Holy Spirit's capacity to flow through us is by lowering ourselves in humility and submitting to the forgiving nature He orders for us to walk in.

The recent passage we just read in James suggests that with confession, we will be forgiven and then be healed. When we know how much God loves us and forgives us, that's when healing begins.

Forgive as you've been forgiven.

"For if you forgive others their trespasses, your Heavenly Father will also forgive you, but if you do not forgive others their trespasses, neither will your Father forgive your trespasses." (Matthew 6:14-15)

"Judge not, and you will not be judged; condemn not, and you will not be condemned; forgive, and you will be forgiven;" (Luke 6:37)

Unforgiveness can delay healing. They are interconnected. Unforgiveness hardens hearts and creates blockages in the soul, which affects the body. We have the

Holy Spirit in us, but in order for Him to flow through properly, our vessels need to be in alignment. As we know, our bodies are temples.

"Do you not know that your bodies are temples of the Holy Spirit, who is in you, whom you have received from God? You are not your own." (1 Corinthians 6:19)

Holding onto unforgiveness turns into bitterness. If we withhold confession of these sins, they will eat away at us.

"Blessed is the one whose transgressions are forgiven, whose sins are covered. Blessed is the one whose sin the LORD does not count against them and in whose spirit is no deceit. When I kept silent, my bones wasted away through my groaning all day long. For day and night your hand was heavy on me; my strength was sapped as in the heat of summer. Then, I acknowledged my sin to you and did not cover up my iniquity. I said, "I will confess my transgressions to the LORD." And you forgave the guilt of my sin." (Psalm 32:1-5)

This testimony shows that with confession and forgiveness, God restores our connection to Him and gives us physical, emotional, and spiritual healing.

"He forgives all my sins and heals all my diseases." (Psalm 103:3)

Prayer:

"Heal me, O LORD, and I shall be healed; Save me, and I shall be saved, For You *are* my praise." (Jeremiah 17:14)

Jesus, I know that Your word promises that all things will work together for good and that You will use all things to glorify You in the end. I lift up my physical and emotional wounds and sickness to You and ask You not just to heal me and take them from me but to use me to shine Your light on others who might be going through something similar. I let go of any unforgiveness I've been harboring. Please release this bitterness from me before it takes root. Soften my heart in humility. I want to be in communion with you. Thank you for forgiving me of my sins and transgressions. Thank You for being the Great Physician and healing Your children in every way. Please use my suffering to have a heart for others suffering similarly and to be a witness to Your goodness and love in all things. In Jesus name, amen!

Chapter 9

Wisdom

"But if any of you lacks wisdom, let him ask of God, who gives to all who generously and without reproach, and it will be given to him." (James 1:5)

"Consider what I say, and may the Lord give you understanding in all things." (2 Timothy 2:7)

God's wisdom vs. the world's wisdom.

One of God's greatest blessings that He has to offer His children is wisdom. The wisdom that God gives isn't like what the world would describe as wise, although it is something so much deeper and more real. He doesn't count people as wise based on their riches or popularity or even accomplishments by a human standard. He counts us wise when we seek Him, obey His word, and follow Him through all things in life.

"The fear of the LORD is the beginning of wisdom, and knowledge of the Holy One is understanding." (Proverbs 9:10)

We must be able to discern what true biblical wisdom is, and the way to filter truth is through scripture. Good thing you're holding a book filled with scripture! Here's a good one:

"Who is wise and understanding among you? Let him show by good conduct that his works are done in the meekness of wisdom. But if you have bitter envy and self-seeking in your hearts, do not boast and lie against the truth. This wisdom does not descend from above, but is earthly, sensual, demonic. For where envy and self-seeking exist, confusion and every evil thing are there." (James 3:13-16)

The world says that someone wise is one who stores up wealth and possessions, has all the right connections, and knows all the right people and so forth. They might also claim the opposite and say someone who lives with nothing and tries to escape this life is wise. God makes it clear that trying to appeal to this world is vanity and foolishness, and seeking Him is the ultimate form of wise living. Also, He gives us our lives to live and blesses us with good things while allowing us to enjoy them. Following Christ is the path to the true wisdom of escaping the traps of this world while also being able to enjoy the good things that this life has to offer. How blessed we are to serve a God who gives true wisdom and gives it abundantly!

Jesus is the ultimate wisdom.

Many people try to find deeper wisdom and end up falling short of what God wants for their lives. They might spend all of their money on books and seminars from people who claim to offer deeper truths or some type of knowledge that can give their lives a sense of purpose. However, God has already given us everything we need in His word, and He reveals all things to us over time as we follow Him more and more. When we have Jesus in our hearts, we have a true wisdom that grows in us and leads us into paths that will ultimately bless us beyond anything we could have imagined.

"But to those called by God to Salvation, both Jews and Gentiles, Christ is the power of God and the wisdom of God." (1 Corinthians 1:24)

"It is because of Him that you are in Christ Jesus, who has become for us the wisdom from God – that is, our righteousness, holiness and redemption." (1 Corinthians 1:30)

"In Him lie hidden all the treasures of wisdom and knowledge." (Colossians 2:3)

We only need to look to Jesus to begin growing in wisdom. He Himself *is* wisdom. Jesus sent the Holy Spirit to help us!

"But the Helper, the Holy Spirit, whom the Father will send in My name, He will teach you all things, and bring to your remembrance all things that I said to you." (John 14:26)

"But when the Helper comes, whom I shall send to you from the Father, the Spirit of truth who proceeds from the Father, He will testify of Me." (John 15:26)

However, when He, the Spirit of truth, has come, He will guide you into all truth; for He will not speak on His own *authority*, but whatever He hears He will speak; and He will tell you things to come. (John 16:13)

And the spirit of the LORD shall rest upon Him, the spirit of wisdom and understanding, the spirit of counsel and might, the spirit of knowledge and of the fear of the LORD. (Isaiah 11:2)

We can see from the scriptures that the spirit of the Lord, the Holy Spirit, is of wisdom and understanding, and He lives in us!

"He is the Holy Spirit who leads into all truth. The world cannot receive Him, because it isn't looking for Him and doesn't recognize Him. But you know Him, because He lives with you now and later will be in you." (John 14:17)

These are the words of Jesus, who promised us that after His death and resurrection, in fact, 50 days after that, the Holy Spirit would come to actually live inside of us believers!

How to gain more wisdom.

Since we have the Holy Spirit, does that mean we have all the wisdom we can ever have already, or must we still grow in that?

King Solomon, the wisest man who lived and will live, when given the opportunity to ask the Lord for anything, asked for wisdom.

"That night, the LORD appeared to Solomon in a dream, and God said, "What do you want? Ask, and I will give it to you!" Solomon replied… "Give me an understanding heart so that I can govern your people well and know the difference between right and wrong. For who by himself is able to govern this great people of yours?" The Lord was pleased that Solomon asked for wisdom. So, God replied, "Because you have asked for wisdom in governing my people with justice and have not asked for a long life or wealth or death of your enemies – I will give you what you asked for! I will give you a wise and understanding heart such as no one else has had or ever will have! And I will also give you what you did not ask for – riches and fame! And if you follow me and obey my decrees and my commands as your father, David, did, I will give you a long life." (1 Kings 3:5, 9-14)

He was even blessed with so much more, too!

Understanding

"Trust in the LORD with all your heart, And lean not on your own understanding." (Proverbs 3:5)

This famous scripture says we should not lean on our own understanding, but that doesn't mean we shouldn't have any understanding! For years, I've mistaken this verse for not being able to seek any understanding, and that was so challenging for me. My natural personality is the type of a chess player. I like to see ahead and plan my moves. But I allowed myself to neglect that because I thought it somehow might be wrong to do so. So, what is it? Well, all throughout the Bible, as we've already read in several passages, it states that God *does* want us to have understanding! It's *His* understanding we must seek. His ways are not our ways, and His thoughts are not our thoughts. But when we seek Him, He loves to speak to us!

"For my thoughts are not your thoughts, neither are your ways my ways," declares the LORD. "As the Heavens are higher than the earth, so are my ways higher than your ways and my thoughts than your thoughts." (Isaiah 55:8-9)

That doesn't mean we can't know the ways and thoughts of God! We are encouraged to seek them out, and He loves to give us insight and revelation.

Daniel answered and said: "Blessed be the name of God forever and ever, For wisdom and might are His. And He changes the times and the seasons; He removes kings and raises up kings; He gives wisdom to wise men, And knowledge to people of understanding. He reveals deep and secret things; He knows what *is* in the darkness, And light swells with Him. I thank You and praise You, O God of my fathers; You have given me wisdom and might, And have no made known to me what we asked of You, For You have made known to us the king's demand." (Daniel 2:20-23)

Daniel didn't sit back quietly and not inquire about the deeper meaning of the king's dream; he simply took it to God and asked the one who knows all. Daniel interpreted the dream with God's wisdom, not his own knowledge or understanding.

"Call to Me, and I will answer you, and show you great and mighty things, which you do not know." (Jeremiah 33:3)

Wisdom Applied

God will give us divine strategy. He will show us the way to go and the blueprints for how to build what He is asking of us. Some notable examples are God giving

Solomon the plans when building the temple and Noah building the ark.

If these men, or any of us, plan to do works for God without partnering with God, the efforts would be in vain.

"Unless the LORD builds the house, they labor in vain who build it; unless the LORD guards the city, The watchman stays awake in vain. It is vain for you to rise up early, to sit up late, to eat the bread of sorrows; For so He gives His beloved sleep." (Psalm 127:1-2)

"But wisdom is proved right by all her children." (Luke 7:35)

These are great reminders to always let God lead!

Wisdom is a responsibility.

When God gives us wisdom, we must always remember that it is to glorify Him and to bring others into a living faith with Jesus Christ. In a world that is lost in darkness and foolishness, wisdom is a very important gift.

However, it can lead some people into pride or arrogance, where they look down on others and assume they are wiser than they are. God gives the gift of wisdom abundantly when we ask Him for this, but we have to always remember to pray and ask for humility at the same time. Wisdom with pride is foolishness in the end, but wisdom with humility is a very powerful weapon in spiritual growth and faith as a believer. God gives wisdom with the responsibility attached that we must use it to always shine His light in this world and help lead the lost back to Him. If we are obedient to this, we will find peace and blessings in our own lives that surpass all understanding, and our lives will be a living testimony to His grace and goodness.

"My son, pay attention to what I say; turn your ear to my words. Do not let them out of your sight, keep them within your heart; for they are life to those who find them and health to one's whole body." (Proverbs 4:20-22)

The word of God gives us life and health. Thank you, Lord, for your word!

This is what the LORD says: "Don't let the wise boast in their wisdom, or the powerful boast in their power, or the rich boast in their riches." (Jeremiah 9:23)

When we are given the spiritual gift of wisdom that leads to material blessings in the natural, we must submit those back to God, as He is the reason we have anything. He gets all the glory, and we should take no credit for accomplishments without Him.

"He who trusts himself is a fool, but one who walks in wisdom will be safe." (Proverbs 28:26)

Thankfully, we have such an easy route to evade foolishness! We simply have the choice to read and obey God's word, and a blessed life will follow.

Prayer:

Heavenly Father, thank You for the wisdom that You give to Your children that is true and everlasting. Please give me the wisdom to follow You in all of my ways and to seek You above all things that this world might have to offer. Thank you also for the good things and gifts that you give me in this life, and please show me how to wisely use them for my benefit and Your glory. In Jesus' name, amen!

Chapter 10

Strength

"I love you, LORD; you are my strength." (Psalm 18:1)

In Jesus, we have the strength of God made available to us! This gift is one that can be applied to all areas of our lives. We aren't doing this life alone; He is with us and He is for us. Although we will face hardships as the trials and tribulations come, the gift of strength is our resource. The joy we read about earlier becomes our strength when we need it! We will have times in life when we need to depend on this, so we thank God for giving it to us. We are to be so grateful even when challenges arise because then we get to use this beautiful strength at its fullest capacity!

"The joy of the Lord is your strength." (Nehemiah 8:10)

"He strengthens the bars of your gates and blesses your people within you." (Psalm 147:13)

God's strength in all circumstances.

The strength that the Lord gives us is something different than what our normal human views of strength might be. It is a strength that isn't dependent on your physical abilities, mental capabilities, or even your emotional state. It is a strength that is in your spirit and that comes directly from the Lord, who creates all things and makes all things happen in perfect harmony. When we seek God, He will answer, and He will give us the strength to get through any circumstance or storm of life. His strength is not one that is flashy or meant to impress the world or show off in any way. It is an often quiet, resolute firmness that will anchor you through any and all circumstances that might occur.

"For I can do everything through Christ, who gives me strength." (Philippians 4:13)

Strength in weakness.

One factor about God's strength that can confuse people is that He makes it clear that His strength is perfected in our weakness. This goes against the logic that most people have that being strong means always being visibly tough or having everything perfect in our lives. However, God loves to use the weak and simple, humble people of this world to glorify Him when they display the divine strength that He gives to those who seek Him. When we have Christ in our hearts and the Holy Spirit is operating through us, we know that there is a power we possess that goes beyond anything human beings can imagine. The very creator of the universe dwells within us and uses us for His purposes and missions in this world. We must always be careful to assume someone is weak and powerless from a worldly standard because they might just be one of the Lord's most powerful warriors.

"That is why, for Christ's sake, I delight in weaknesses, in insults, in hardships, in persecutions, in difficulties. For when I am weak, then I am strong." (2 Corinthians 12:10)

"Do not fear, for I am with you; do not be afraid, for I am your God. I will strengthen you, I will also help you, I will also uphold you with my righteous right hand." (Isaiah 41:10)

"God is our refuge and strength, a very present help in trouble." (Psalm 46:1)

"He gives strength to the weary and increases the power of the weak. Even youths grow tired and weary, and young men stumble and fall; but those who hope in the LORD will renew their strength. They will soar on wings like eagles; they will run and not grow weary, they will walk and not be faint." (Isaiah 40:29-31)

Build up the strengths in others!

In Christ, we are all one Body. That means that we all play our own unique roles and have our own special gifts, but we use them in unity to help one another and to advance the Kingdom of Christ on Earth. God gives us all different strengths and weaknesses, and we must always be aware of how we can encourage one another and build up one another's strengths. For instance, if you are good at teaching but your brother or sister in Christ is good with counseling, remember that everyone has a special role to play in the

Body of Christ. Those talents complement one another in our common goal of spreading the Gospel and helping the lost to be saved. When we encourage one another in love, we not only help that person to recognize their worth and unique talents, but we also build up the entire Body of Christ as a whole and strengthen us all!

"And He Himself gave some to be Apostles, some Prophets, some Evangelists, and some Pastors and Teachers, for the equipping of the saints for the work of ministry, for the edifying of the body of Christ." (Ephesians 4:11-12)

"So, encourage each other and build each other up, just as you are already doing." (1 Thessalonians 5:11)

Prayer:

Lord Jesus, please give me the strength for today that can only come from You and Your power. Thank You for using my weaknesses to glorify You and for making me strong in ways that I never imagined. Please continue to build Your strength in me and make me Holy in Your sight. Thank You that when the world sees me in weakness, you see me as Your warrior in training. In Jesus' name, amen!

Final

I never stop giving thanks for you as I remember you in my prayers, I pray that the God of our Lord Jesus Christ, the glorious Father, would give you the Spirit of wisdom and revelation in the knowledge of Him. I pray that the eyes of your heart may be enlightened so that you may know what is the hope of His calling, what is the wealth of His glorious inheritance in the saints, and what is the immeasurable greatness of His power toward us who believe, according to the might working of His strength. (Ephesians 1:16-19)

love,

Shannon Klein

About the Author

Shannon Klein currently resides in Las Vegas, NV, while frequently traveling to share the love of Jesus all over the world. Shannon's life is a tapestry of diverse experiences, woven together by a deep passion for ministry and a heart for serving others. Growing up on a small island, Shannon found peace in the simple joys of life and beauty of nature, while longing to reach the nations. At 15 years old, she graduated high school and went to college at USC to study Music Industry and Japanese. Her unique upbringing shaped her easygoing yet purpose-driven approach to life, blending joy and reflection with a heart for deeper meaning.

Shannon has had a personal relationship with Jesus since before she could remember, and at a very young age, she knew she was called to lead and serve others. Her interesting career path has taken her from being a poker player to a comedian, experiences that not only sharpened her wit and strategic thinking but also taught her the importance of connecting with people from all walks of life. Her comedic authenticity allows her to relate to others in a unique way, while poker helped her cultivate patience, resilience, and discernment – qualities that have served her well in her ministry work.

Now, Shannon is pursuing a Master of Theology degree and works in full-time ministry. With an apostolic calling, she embodies a genuine love for people and is driven to spread hope and inspire others to walk in their fulfilling missions. Her ministry is not just a vocation but a deep-seated passion to serve those in need, and she brings her gifts of humor, insight, and leadership to every meeting.

As an author, Shannon invites readers to encounter the love of God for themselves and to hear His voice on their own. Whether on the road or at home, she lives with an openness for the Holy Spirit to lead, guide, and direct her day. Her understanding of the salvation and invitation to Heaven is not only for eternity, but also in the here and now, and she encourages others to walk in this freedom so they too can see the goodness of the Lord in the land of the living.

www.ingramcontent.com/pod-product-compliance
Lightning Source LLC
Chambersburg PA
CBHW071716040426
42446CB00011B/2089